Kissing the Shoreline

QUOTES AND REFLECTIONS TO LIVE BY

JULIE SAFFRIN

Book Cover design by Katie Brink, brinkgirl.com
Author Photo: Barbara Marshak
Book Cover photo from depositphoto.com by pwollinga

Scripture references are taken from the following sources:

Ottertail Press, PO Box 48313, Minneapolis, Minnesota 55448

ISBN-10: 0692244417   ISBN-13: 978-0692244418

DEDICATION

To my husband Rick,

sons, Sam, Joe and Jake

and to Hallie, Anna, and Jenny

You have changed my life and

I am honored to know and love you

CONTENTS

JULIE SAFFRIN

FOREWORD

In business, one needs to "go to the mattresses" — at least Tom Hanks said so to Meg Ryan in *You've Got Mail*. In my case, as a writer where observations, ponderings and creating turns-of-phrases are golden, I go to my quote book. Somewhere in the process of reading and re-reading these quotes, I come away influenced and changed. This book is a compilation of my favorites.

On social media, you'll find walls and boards put to beautiful images. Why do we love Facebook posts or Pinterest boards with a good quote? A great quote and a beautiful image is visible music. Nature inspires and a great quote refuels. Paired together, they help us begin tired determinations again.

Love Song to J. Alfred Prufrock is a poem by T. S. Eliot about a man with a dilemma. He spends his life thinking about a girl to whom he is attracted. He wonders whether or not he has the right to intrude upon another's life. He asks at the end of the poem, "Do I dare disturb the universe?"

My little book is filled with words from people who, because they put their thoughts down, because they disturbed the universe, have helped me step, stone by stone, through life. I go to them when I need a pick-me-up, a chuckle, or a shove. Their turns-of-phrases fill me with "word courage." They give me the courage to write. I tell myself that if the people quoted here dared their words into existence then why shouldn't I dare to speak or write mine?

My hope is that the words found here will make you contemplative, cause you an *a-ha* moment, or challenge you.

Memorize one or two, so when the hard times come, or you need a dose of humor (my favorite is Dolly Parton's take on beauty), you give yourself a better day. Commit enough of them to memory and you'll hear them whisper to you in the wind or tickle your ear, and the words will remind you to keep your eyes on your goal as you work to make your dreams into reality.

While compiling this book, I came across a quote by Sarah Kay:

> *Because there's nothing more beautiful*
> *than the way the ocean refuses to stop kissing the shoreline,*
> *no matter how many times it's sent away.*

Its beautiful message expresses two metaphors for me. Firstly, I envision the ocean to be that of a loving God Who is in constant pursuit of us. No matter how many times we, like the shoreline, send Him away from being in our lives, we will always be God-chased, for we cannot outrun Him.

Secondly, Kay's words apply to you and me. It is an appeal, a call to each one of us, no matter how many times we are rejected, to keep sending our dreams and ideas into the shoreline we call the universe. Thankfully, for you and me, it's the antithesis to Eliot's *Prufrock*.

So, go disturb the universe, as only you are meant to do.

With gratitude,

Julie Saffrin

What is life for?

It is for you.

— Abraham Maslow

JULIE SAFFRIN

ABILITY

John Wooden

Ability may get you to the top, but it takes character to keep you there.

Robert Schuller

Every achiever I have ever met says, "My life turned around when I began to believe in me."

ACCOMPLISHMENT

Edmund Burke

No man makes a greater mistake than he who does nothing because he knows it is not everything.

Julia Cameron

Finish something.

ACTION

Og Mandino

I will act now. I will act now. I will act now. Henceforth, I will repeat these words each hour, each day, every day, until the words become as much a habit as my breathing, and the action which follows becomes as instinctive as the blinking of my eyelids. With these words I can condition my mind to perform every action necessary for my success. I will act now. I will repeat these words again and again and again. I will walk where failures fear to walk. I will work when failures seek rest. I will act now for now is all I have. Tomorrow is the day reserved for the labor of the lazy. I am not lazy. Tomorrow is the day when the failure will succeed. I am not a failure. I will act now. Success will not wait. If I delay, success will become wed to another and lost to me forever. This is the time. This is the place. I am the person.

ADVERSITY

Walt Disney

All the adversity I've had in my life, all my troubles and obstacles, have strengthened me ... You may not realize it when it happens, but a kick in the teeth may be the best thing in the world for you.

Arthur Golden

Adversity is like a strong wind. It tears away from us all but the things that cannot be torn, so that we see ourselves as we really are. From *Memoirs of a Geisha*

AGE

Groucho Marx

Age is not a particularly interesting subject. Anyone can get old. All you have to do is live long enough.

Rosalind Russell

Keep my mind free from the recital of endless details; Give me wings to get to the point. Seal my lips on aches and pains. They are increasing, and love of rehearsing them is becoming sweeter as the years go by. — A prayer petition Frederick Brisson found in his wife's prayer book after she had died. Rosalind had several cancerous tumors and rheumatoid arthritis.

ANALOGY

Julie Saffrin

I asked my Cornish friend if he wanted to go the Cornish festival in Wisconsin while in the United States. He said, "That's a bit like carrying coals to Newcastle, innit?"

Horace aka Quintus Horatius Flaccus

An American translation of my friend's repartee comes from: "As crazy as hauling timber into the wood. *Satires, book 1, satire X, 1, 34*

APPRECIATION

Audrey Hepburn

Pick the day. Enjoy it - to the hilt. The day as it comes. People as they come ... The past, I think, has helped me appreciate the present, and I don't want to spoil any of it by fretting about the future.

Author Unknown

Living life in a posture of appreciation is the best way.

Steve Maraboli

One of the most spiritual things you can do is embrace your humanity. Connect with those around you today. Say, "I love you," "I'm sorry," "I appreciate you," "I'm proud of you" ... whatever you're feeling. Send random texts, write a cute note, embrace your truth and share it ... cause a smile today for someone else ... and give plenty of hugs.

Mary Anne Radmacher

Live with intention. Walk to the edge. Listen hard. Practice wellness. Play with abandon. Laugh. Choose with no regret. Appreciate your friends. Continue to learn. Do what you love.

Robert Louis Stevenson

The man is a success who has lived well, laughed often, and loved much; who has gained the respect of intelligent men and the love of children; who has filled his niche and accomplished his task; who leaves the world better than he found it, whether by an improved poppy, a perfect poem, or a rescued soul; who never lacked appreciation of earth's beauty or failed to express it; who looked for the best in others and gave the best he had.

ARCHITECTURE

Johann Wolfgang von Goethe

I call architecture frozen music.

Frank Lloyd Wright

The physician can bury his mistakes, but the architect can only advise his client to plant vines.

ART

Author Unknown

The journey of art is a million miles, but the most important distance is the last inch.

Roy H. Williams

Every beginner's solution is to put an "attention getter" into the ad. Bright colors, loud noises, exclamation marks, and crazy stunts are the sad little attentions-getters most often used. The effect on your beautiful customer is much the same as sneaking up behind her and shouting, "WATCH OUT!" Is this any way to start a romance? I vote for seduction ... You must offer her a thought more interesting than the thought that currently occupies her mind. This does not require shouting. This requires art.

ATTITUDE

James Branch Coberl

The optimist proclaims that we live in the best of all possible worlds. The pessimist fears this is true.

BABY

Martin Farquhar Tupper

A baby in the house is a wellspring of pleasure, a messenger of peace and love, a resting place for innocence on earth, a link between angels and men.

BEAUTY

Debra Antone

Some days you wear a costume. Some days you wear a hat.

Coco Chanel

You don't need money. You need richness of heart, and elegance.

Jean Kerr

I'm tired of all this nonsense about beauty being only skin-deep. That's deep enough. What do you want? An adorable pancreas?

Dolly Parton

It costs a lot of money to look this cheap.

BEGIN

Marie Beyon Ray

Begin doing what you want to do now. We are not living in eternity. We have only this moment, sparkling like a star in our hand — and melting like a snowflake.

Liz Smith

Begin somewhere. You cannot build a reputation on what you intend to do.

BELONGING

Michelle Montaigne

The first thing in the world is knowing how to belong to oneself.

BIRTHDAY

Dr. Suess

A Wasn't just isn't. He just isn't present. But you...You ARE YOU! And, now isn't that pleasant!

Dr. Suess

Today you are You, that is truer than true. There is no one alive who is Youer than You.

BITTERNESS

Max Lucado

Bitterness is the trap that snares the hunter.

BLESSINGS

C. H. Spurgeon

Faith is the only way whereby thou canst obtain blessings. From *Morning and Evening*

BOOKS

Anton Chekhov

When I am reading a book, whether wise or silly, it seems to be alive and talking to me.

Albert Guéar

The great books exist, not to hem us in, but to help us break our bonds.

John Milton

A good book is the precious life-blood of a master spirit, embalmed and treasured up on purpose to a life beyond life.

CALM

Keep Calm and carry on. — Motivational poster produced by the British government in 1939.

CAREERS

Gary Sinise

Careers, like rockets, don't always take off on schedule. The key is to keep working the engines.

CHANCE

Louis Pasteur

Chance favors only the prepared mind.

CHANGE

Chinese Proverb

Better to light a candle than to curse the darkness.

Anne Frank

How wonderful it is that nobody need wait a single moment before starting to improve the world.

Gandhi

You must be the change you wish to see in the world.

Steve Jobs

Here's to the crazy ones. The misfits. The rebels. The troublemakers. The round pegs in the square holes. The ones who see things differently. They're not fond of rules. And they have no respect for the status quo. You can quote them, disagree with them, glorify or vilify them. About the only thing you can't do is ignore them. Because they change things. They invent. They imagine. They heal. They explore. They create. They inspire. They push the human race forward. Maybe they have to be crazy. While some see them as the crazy ones, we see genius. Because the people who are crazy enough to think they can change the world, are the ones who do.

Rosalind Russell

A doctor will tell you not to worry about things you can't change; it's like trying to affect the tides. From *Life's a Banquet*

Julie Saffrin

Dream. Believe. Start. Reach. Do. Change the way you look at the world and the world changes the way it looks at you.

CHARACTER

Helen Keller

Character cannot be developed in ease and quiet. Only through experience of trial and suffering can the soul be strengthened, ambition inspired, and success achieved.

CHRISTIANITY

G. K. Chesterton

The Christian ideal has not been tried and found wanting. It has been found difficult; and left untried. From *What's Wrong with the World*

Steve Trewartha

Christianity is the true story that communicates the truth of God to people, and to believe in and follow Christ is to join one's own life to that narrative. Christianity is not merely a set of doctrines to which we assent, or a self-help guide to a more satisfying life, but a powerful story that invites us to live rich lives with ultimate purpose.

CHRISTMAS

Julie Saffrin

We go to the hospital to visit a newborn baby and notice family resemblances. We say, "Oh, your baby looks just like his father or just like his mother." I like to think of the manger in Bethlehem as similar to that of a maternity ward. There is a newborn baby in Bethlehem. He looks just like His Father. He looks like His mother. He looks like us. And, we, bearing relation to God, look like Him.

COMPASSION AND CONVICTIONS

Rick Warren

Our culture has accepted two huge lies. The first is that if you disagree with someone's lifestyle, you must fear or hate them. The second is that to love someone means you agree with everything they believe or do. Both are nonsense. You don't have to compromise convictions to be compassionate.

CONFESSION

Pastor: Almighty God, our Maker and Redeemer, we poor sinners confess unto Thee that we are by nature sinful and unclean, and that we have sinned against Thee by thought, word, and deed. Wherefore we flee for refuge to Thine infinite mercy, seeking and imploring Thy grace for the sake of our Lord Jesus Christ.

Congregation: O most merciful God, who has given Thine only begotten Son to die for us, have mercy upon us and for His sake grant us remission of all our sins; and by the Holy Spirit increase in us true knowledge of Thee and of Thy will and true obedience to Thy Word, to the end, that by Thy grace we may come to everlasting life; through Jesus Christ, our Lord. Amen. From *The old Lutheran red hymnal*

CONFLICT-RESOLUTION QUESTION

Ask, "What do I need to do to resolve this? It's not my heart's desire to be offensive. If I have offended you in any way I apologize." Once the conflict is resolved and you heal from it, God will give you your next assignment. — Overheard conversation

CONFORMING

Rita Mae Brown

The reward for conformity was that everyone liked you except yourself.

CONSTANT

Rumer Godden

"Constant" does not merely mean "perpetual;" its larger meaning is faithfulness, firmness of purpose, resolution. From *The Will to Write*, May 1985 *The Writer*

CONTENTMENT

Marcus Tullius Cicero

To be content with what we possess is the greatest and most secure of riches.

CORNISH BLESSING

Cornish Christian Mission

Deep peace of the Running Wave to you; Deep peace of the Flowing Air to you; Deep peace of the Quiet Earth to you; Deep peace of the Shining Stars to you; Deep peace of the Son of Peace to you.

COURAGE

Raymond Lindquist

Courage is the power to let go of the familiar.

Mary Anne Radmacher

Courage doesn't always roar. Sometimes courage is the little voice at the end of the day that says, "I'll try again tomorrow."

Mark Twain

Courage is resistance to fear, mastery of fear — not absence of fear. Except a creature be part coward it is not a compliment to say it is brave.

CROSS CULTURAL APPRECIATION

Yo Yo Ma

When you learn something from people or from a culture, you accept it as a gift, and it is your lifelong commitment to preserve it and build on it.

CURIOUS

Albert Einstein

I have no special talents. I am only passionately curious.

DAY

Author Unknown

Normal day, let me be aware of the treasure you are.

Marcel Proust

The time which we have at our disposal every day is elastic; the passions that we feel expand it; those we inspire contract it; and habit fills up what remains.

DEATH

George Carlin

If no one knows when a person is going to die, how can we say, "He died prematurely"?

DECISION

Martin Luther King, Jr.

There comes a time when one must take a position that is neither safe, nor politic, nor popular, but he must take it because conscience tells him it is right.

DESERT YEARS

Luci Shaw

I think of these desert years of mine, not of my choosing. Maybe if it were all smooth and comfortable, if my pride and professionalism were defining life for me, God's steel-quiet, penetrating word would have been lost in the babble and sheen of success.

DESPAIR

Betsy ten Boom

There is no pit where God is not deeper still.

Henry David Thoreau

Most men lead lives of quiet desperation.

DESTINY

William Jennings Bryant

Destiny is not a matter of chance, but a matter of choice. It is not a thing to be waited for. It is a thing to be achieved.

Jean De La Fontaine

A person often meets his destiny on the road he took to avoid it.

Barbara Marshak

Like some sorry animal caught in a trap, he was destined to live under his father's sordid rules. The realization hit him swift and hard, like an angry rodeo bull knocking him into the ground. From *Seeds of Salton*

DETERMINATION

Julie Saffrin

Help me not to let my "I'm going to," turn into "I never did." From a prayer said in 2006, halfway through obtaining a bachelor's degree as a middle-aged adult.

DIETS

Dolly Parton

I've tried every diet in the book. I tried some that weren't in the book. I tried eating the book. It tasted better than most of the diets.

DIGNITY

Viktor Frankl

What you have experienced, no power on earth can take from you. From *Man's Search for Meaning*

DILIGENCE

G. K. Chesterton

A man must love a thing very much if he not only practices it without any hope of fame or money, but even practices it without any hope of doing it well.

DIRECTION

Anthony Robbins

Concentrate on where you want to go, not on what you fear.

DISCIPLINE

Thomas Henry Huxley

Perhaps the most valuable result of all education is the ability to make yourself do the thing you have to do, when it ought to be done, whether you like it or not; it is the first lesson that ought to be learned; and however early a man's training begins, it is probably the last lesson that he learns thoroughly.

Joseph de Maistre

There are no easy methods of learning difficult things; the method is to close the door, give out that you are not at home, and work.

DISCOVERIES

Marcel Proust

The real voyage of discovery consists not in seeking new landscapes but in having new eyes.

DIVORCE

Jean Kerr

Being divorced is like being hit by a Mack truck. If you live through it you start looking very carefully to the right and to the left.

DOG VERSUS A CAT

Author Unknown

The difference between a dog and a cat is that a dog has a master. A cat has a staff.

DOING

Mother Teresa

I don't do big things. I do small things with big love.

DREAMS

Sarah Ban Breathnach

As long as you're actively pursuing your dream with a practical plan, you're still achieving, even if it feels as though you're going nowhere fast. It's been my experience that at the very moment I feel like giving up, I'm only one step from a breakthrough. Hang on long enough and circumstances will change, too. Trust in yourself, your dream and spirit.

Cinderella

Have faith in your dreams and someday, your rainbow will come shining through. No matter how your heart is grieving, if you keep believing, the dream that you wish will come true.

Henry David Thoreau

Go confidently in the direction of your dreams. Live the life you've imagined.

Dale Turner

Dreams are renewable. No matter what our age or condition, there are still untapped possibilities within us and new beauty waiting to be born.

William Butler Yeats

But I, being poor, have only my dreams, I have spread my dreams under your feet; Tread softly because you tread on my dreams. From *He Wishes for the Cloths of Heaven*

DUTY

Author Unknown

Duty makes us do things well, but love makes us do them beautifully.

ENCOURAGEMENT

Judy Garland

Always be a first-rate version of yourself instead of a second-rate version of somebody else.

Rose Kennedy

Birds sing after a storm; why shouldn't people feel as free to delight in whatever remains to them?

William Arthur Ward

Flatter me, and I may not believe you. Criticize me, and I may not like you. Ignore me, and I may not forgive you. Encourage me, and I will not forget you.

ENDURANCE

Italian Proverb

He who endures conquers.

ENTERTAINMENT

Groucho Marx

I've had a wonderful time, but this wasn't it.

EPITAPH

Dorothy Parker

Excuse my dust.

ERRORS

Roger von Oech

If you make an error, use it as a stepping stone to a new idea you might not have otherwise discovered.

EVIDENCE OF GOD ON EARTH

Elizabeth Barrett Browning

Earth's crammed with heaven, And every common bush afire with God; But only he who sees, takes off his shoes, The rest sit round it and pluck blackberries. From *Aurora Leigh*

EVIL

Edmund Burke

All that is necessary for evil to prosper is for good men to do nothing.

FAILURE

William D. Brown

Failure is an event, never a person.

Robert Butterworth

Don't focus on the days when you failed. Focus on all of the days when you won. Keep a chart, monitor your successes, and don't give up!

Confucius

Our greatest glory is not in ever failing but in rising every time we fail.

Henry Ford

Failure is only the opportunity to begin again more intelligently.

Japanese Proverb

Fall seven times; stand up eight.

FAITH

Anonymous

Faith is daring the soul to go beyond what the eyes can see.

FAITH AND DOUBT

Augustine

Faith is to believe what you do not yet see; the reward for this faith is to see what you believe.

Fyodor Dostoyevsky

My hosannas have come through whirlwinds of doubt.

FAITHFULNESS

Hudson Taylor

A little thing is a little thing, but faithfulness in a little thing is a big thing.

FEAR

Pope John XXIII

Consult not your fears but your hopes and your dreams. Think not about your frustrations, but about your unfulfilled potential. Concern yourself not with what you tried and failed in, but with what it is still possible for you to do.

FINDING YOUR VOICE

John Grisham

In life, finding a voice is speaking and living the truth. Each of you is an original. Each of you has a distinctive voice. When you find it, your story will be told. You will be heard.

FLOPS

Rosalind Russell

Flops are part of life's menu, and I'm never a girl to miss out on any of the courses. From *Life's a Banquet*

FLY

Guy Murchie

She was built like a whale, for cargo and comfort. Ninety-four feet long and full-bellied, with wide tail flukes that could ease her nose up or down at the merest nudge of her controls. Her sinews and nerves were four-and-a-half miles of steel cable and insulated copper wire. Her brain was a set of instruments tended by radio waves, inertia, magnetic force, and atmospheric pressure, and all pivoted on sapphires and crystals of rare hardness. She was Number 896, one of the original C-54s, the famous flying freighters designed especially for ocean transport — perhaps the most widely used long-range weight-carrying airplane to appear in the decades since man taught metal to fly. From *Song of the Sky*

FORGET

William Durant

Forget past mistakes. Forget failures. Forget everything except what you're going to do now, and do it. — Founder of General Motors

FORGIVENESS

Ritu Ghatourney

He who cannot forgive others destroys a bridge over which he himself must pass.

Luis Palau

Clara Barton, founder of the American Red Cross, was reminded one day of a vicious deed someone had done to her years before. "Don't you remember it?" her friend asked. "No," came Barton's reply. "I distinctly remember forgetting it." From *Experiencing God's Forgiveness*

FRIENDSHIP

Marita Bonner

She did not talk to people as if they were strange hard shells she had to crack open to get inside. She talked as if she were already in the shell. In their very shell.

Virginia Froehle

Friendship is the warm cloak we wear over our winter lives. Friends wrap us with affirmation, enfold us with understanding, and protect us against the cold winds of hostility and criticism. Friendship is the cool breeze of our summer lives. Friends sail along with us in our pleasure, enjoy the sun of our successes, breathe carefulness upon us. From *Loving Yourself More*

C. S. Lewis

In friendship ... we think we have chosen our peers. In reality a few years' difference in the dates of our births, a few more miles between certain houses, the choice of one university instead of another ... the accident of a topic being raised or not raised at a first meeting — any of these chances might have kept us apart. But, for a Christian, there are, strictly speaking no chances. A secret master of ceremonies has been at work. Christ, who said to the disciples, "Ye have not chosen me, but I have chosen you," can truly say to every group of Christian friends, "Ye have not chosen one another but I have chosen you for one another." The friendship is not a reward for our discriminating and good taste in finding one another out. It is the instrument by which God reveals to each of us the beauties of others. From *The Four Loves*

Helen Keller

My friends have made the story of my life. In a thousand ways, they have turned my limitations into beautiful privileges and enabled me to walk serene and happy in the shadows cast by my deprivation.

A. A. Milne

If you live to be a hundred, I want to live to be a hundred minus one day, so I never have to live without you.

A. A. Milne

"Pooh?" "Yes, Piglet." "Oh nothing. I just wanted to know you were there."

FUTURE

M. Louise Hawkins

And I said to the man who stood at the gate of the year: "Give me light that I may tread safely into the unknown." And he replied: "Go out into the darkness, and put your hand into the hand of God. That shall be to you better than light, and safer than the known way."

Norman Vincent Peale

Any fact facing us is not as important as our attitude toward it, for that determines our success or failure.

GOAL-SETTING

Author Unknown

A knowledge of the path cannot be substituted for putting one foot in front of the other.

Henry Ford

Obstacles are those frightful things you see when you take your eyes off your goal.

Julius Irving

Goals determine what you are going to be.

T. E. Lawrence

All men dream, but not equally. Those who dream by night in the dusty recesses of their minds, wake in the day to find that it was vanity: but the dreamers of the day are dangerous men, for they may act on their dreams with open eyes, to make them possible.

Gordon MacDonald

The Old Testament scribe Ezra believed in the growth of the mind. "And Ezra set himself to study the law of the Lord, to do it, and to teach its statutes in all Israel." The order is worth noting: He studied. He did what he learned. He shared what was worthwhile" ... And because his mind and spirit were full, God tapped Ezra for the gigantic task of leading a large task force of men across the wilderness to rebuild Jerusalem. From *Ordering Your Private World*

GOOD VERSUS GREAT

Michael Ruhlman

Great is the enemy of good. When surgeons strive for greatness, they can cause harm when they might otherwise not have harmed had they simply strived for good. I've worked with the greatest perfectionists there is in the cooking world, and I love that hunt for the perfect sauce, the perfect custard, but here I'm after good. Only when we know good can we begin to inch up from good to excellent. From *Ratio: The Simple Codes Behind The Craft of Everyday Cooking*

GRATITUDE

Andre Agassi

The scoreboard said I lost today, but what the scoreboard doesn't say is what it is I have found. Over the last 21 years, I have found loyalty. You have pulled for me on the court and also in life. I found inspiration. You have willed me to succeed, sometimes even in my lowest moments, and I've found generosity. You have given me your shoulders to stand on to reach for my dreams, dreams I could never have reached without you. — To the fans after the last match of his professional tennis career

Melody Beattie

Gratitude unlocks the fullness of life. It turns what we have into enough, and more. It turns denial into acceptance, chaos to order, confusion to clarity. It can turn a meal into a feast, a house into a home, a stranger into a friend. Gratitude makes sense of our past, brings peace for today, and creates a vision for tomorrow.

Luci Swindoll

The gratitude-filled woman has learned happiness is not about having what she wants, but wanting what she has.

GRIEF

Dean Koontz

Grief can destroy you — or focus you. You can decide a relationship was all for nothing if it had to end in death, and you alone. Or you can realize that every moment of it had more meaning than you dared to recognize at the time, so much meaning it scared you, so you just lived, just took for granted the love and laughter of each day, and didn't allow yourself to consider the sacredness of it. But when it's over and you're alone, you begin to see that it wasn't just a movie and a dinner together, not just watching sunsets together, not just scrubbing a floor or washing dishes together or worrying over a high electric bill. It was everything. It was the why of life, every event and precious moment of it. The answer to the mystery of existence is the love you shared sometimes so imperfectly, and when the loss wakes you to the deeper beauty of it, to the sanctity of it, you can't get off your knees not by the weight of the loss but by gratitude for what preceded the loss. And the ache is always there, but one day not the emptiness, because to nurture the emptiness, to take solace in it, is to disrespect the gift of life. From *Odd Thomas*

Dawn Clifton Tripp

As she walks, she can feel the leak in her heart. She holds her breath and practices growing still, so she can navigate the dimensions of the tear. From *Moontide*

William Shakespeare

Grief makes one hour ten.

GROWTH

ChocoWit saying

Expanded horizons inspire new growth.

GUIDANCE

Jane Kise

God's guidance is more like a lamp unto our feet than a lighthouse beaming far into the future. From *Finding and Following God's Will*

HAPPINESS

Henry Ward Beecher

Blessed are the happiness makers.

Dale Carnegie

Happiness doesn't depend upon you who are or what you have; it depends solely upon what you think.

Lydia Maria Child

An effort made for the happiness of others lifts above ourselves.

Jodi Hills

In a moment of happiness is always a good place to catch yourself.

Rick Warren

The only really happy people are those who have learned how to serve.

HATRED

Max Lucado

Hatred is the rabid dog that turns on its owner.

HEART

Charles Dickens

Have a heart that never hardens, a temper that never tires, and a touch that never hurts.

Margaret Thatcher

To wear your heart on your sleeve isn't a very good plan. You should wear it inside where it functions best. — In an interview with Barbara Walters, 1987

HISTORY

Blackie Sherrod

History must repeat itself because we pay such little attention to it the first time.

HOPE

Samuel Smiles

Hope is the companion of power, and mother of success; for who so hopes strongly has within him the gift of miracles.

HOW TO LIVE

Jim Eliot

Wherever you are, be all there. Live to the hilt any situation you believe to be the will of God.

HUMILITY

Golda Meir

Don't be so humble; You're not that great.

HYPOCRISY

A word derived from the Greek word for "stage-acting."

IDEAS

Rainer Maria Rilke

Leave to your opinions their own quiet undisturbed development, which like all progress, must come from deep within and cannot be pressed or hurried by anything.

IDENTITY

Julie Saffrin

Scripture says we bear His likeness (Psalm 17:15). I seek to live in the mindset of God, who says I am made in His image rather than to live like I bear no resemblance to Him.

IMPORTANCE OF STILLNESS

William Wordsworth

... With an eye made quiet by the power, of harmony, and the deep power of joy, we see into the life of things. From *Lines Composed a Few Miles Above Tintern Abbey*

INCARNATION AND CHRISTMAS

C. S. Lewis

The central miracle asserted by Christmas is the Incarnation. They say God became Man. Every other miracle prepares for this, or exhibits this or results from this. Just as every natural event is the manifestation at a particular place and moment of Nature's total character, so every particular Christian miracle manifests at a place and moment the character and significance of the Incarnation. There is no question in Christianity of arbitrary interferences just scattered about. From *Miracles*

INERTIA

Justina Chen

Inertia is so easy — don't fix what's not broken. Leave well enough alone. So we end up accepting what is broken, mistaking complaining for action, procrastinating for deliberation. From *North of Beautiful*

Will Rogers

Even if you are on the right track, you'll get run over if you just sit there.

INVISIBLENESS

Dawn Clifton Tripp

She lives in town for a good six months before they see her. She thins herself into the trees and crawls between rocks like an idea before its time, which takes up no space, and then if out of nowhere, explodes into the mind. From *Moontide*

IRISH BLESSING

A sunbeam to warm you, a moonbeam to charm you, a sheltering angel, so nothing can harm you.

May love and laughter light your days and warm your heart and home, may good and faithful friends be yours wherever you may roam, may peace and plenty bless your world with joy that long endures, may all life's passing seasons bring the best to you and yours.

May the leprechauns dance over your bed and bring you sweet dreams. May you always walk in sunshine. May you never want for more. May Irish angels rest their wings right beside your door.

May the road rise up to meet you. May the wind be always at your back. May the sunshine warm upon your face, and the rain fall soft upon your fields, and until we meet again, may God hold you in the palm of His hand.

JOY

Denise Levertov

That's joy, it's always a recognition, the known appearing fully itself, and more itself than one knew. From *Matins*

JUDGING

Jonathan Bender

I only critique you if you pay me.

Emily Dickinson

This is my letter to the world, That never wrote to me, — The simple news that Nature told, With tender majesty. Her message is committed, To hands I cannot see; For love of her sweet countrymen, Judge tenderly of me!

KEEPING AT IT

Ray Kroc

Press on. Nothing in the world can take the place of persistence. — Founder of McDonalds

KINDNESS

Author Unknown

A kindness done today is the surest way to a brighter tomorrow.

Sir James Matthew Barrie

Shall we make a new rule of life from tonight: always to try to be a little kinder than is necessary? From *The Little White Bird*

James Dickey

More kindness will do nothing less. Than save every sleeping one. And nightwalking one. Of us. My life belongs to the world. I will do what I can. From *The Strength of Fields*

James Keller

A candle loses nothing by lighting another candle.

Mother Teresa

Let no one ever come to you without leaving better and happier. Be the living expression of God's kindness: kindness in your face, kindness in your eyes, and kindness in your smile.

John Watson

Be kind, for everyone you meet is fighting a hard battle.

THE KINGDOM OF GOD

C. S. Lewis

Law, in his terrible, cool voice, said ... "If you have not chosen the Kingdom of God, it will make in the end no difference what you have chosen instead." Does it matter to a man dying in a desert by which choice of route he missed the only well? From *The Weight of Glory*

LAND OF HEART'S DESIRE

William Butler Yeats

Where beauty has no ebb, decay no flood, But joy is wisdom, Time an endless song.

LEADERS

Vince Lombardi

Leaders are not born. They are made. They are made just like anything else ... through hard work. That's the price we have to pay to achieve that goal or any goal.

Dolly Parton

If your actions create a legacy that inspires others to dream more, learn more, do more and become more, then you are an excellent leader.

Tom Peters

Leaders don't create followers, they create more leaders.

LEARNING FROM OTHERS

Douglas Adams

Human beings, who are almost unique in having the ability to learn from the experiences of others, are also remarkable for their apparent disinclination to do so.

LETTERS

Phyllis Theroux

To send a letter is a good way to go somewhere without moving anything but your heart.

LIFE

Maya Angelou

Life loves the liver of it.

Arthur Ashe

From what we get, we can make a living; what we give, however, makes a life.

Author Unknown

Every step is the journey.

Leo Buscaglia

Life is a paradise for those who love many things with a passion.

Walter Cronkite

And that's the way it is. — Sign-off sentence, CBS Evening News

Max Ehrmann

Go placidly amid the noise and the haste, and remember what peace there may be in silence. As far as possible without surrender, be on good terms with all persons. Speak your truth quietly and clearly, and listen to others, even the dull and ignorant; they too have their story. Be yourself. Especially do not feign affection. Neither be cynical about love – for in the face of all aridity and disenchantment is it perennial as the grass. Take kindly the counsel of the years, gracefully surrendering the things of youth. Nurture strength of spirit to shield you from misfortune. But do not distress yourself with imaginings. Many fears are born of fatigue and loneliness. Beyond a wholesome discipline, be gentle with yourself. You are a child of the universe no less than the trees and the stars; you have a right to be here. And whether or not it is clear to you, no doubt the universe is unfolding as it should. Therefore be at peace with God, whatever you conceive Him to be, and whatever your labors and aspirations, in the noisy confusion of life keep peace with your soul. With all its sham, drudgery and broken dreams, it is still a beautiful world. From *Desiderata: A Poem for a Way of Life*

William E. Gladstone

Be inspired with the belief that life is a great and noble calling; not a mean and groveling thing that we are to shuffle through as we can, but an elevated and lofty destiny.

Teri Johnson

Our life is a garden; whatever we feed and focus on grows. From *Overcoming the Nevers*

Sister Helen Kelly

Choose Life! Only that and always! At whatever risk, to let life leak out, to let it wear away by the mere passage of time. To withhold giving and spending it ... is to choose nothing.

Groucho Marx

Some days you're the dog; some days you're the hydrant.

Abraham Maslow

What is life for? It is for you.

Julie Saffrin

There's more to life than reducing the broth.

Albert Schweitzer

Anyone who has accustomed himself to regard the life of any living creature as worthless is in danger of arriving also at the idea of worthless human lives.

Jennifer Weiner

I've learned a lot this year. I learned that things don't always turn out the way you planned, or the way you think they should. And I've learned that there are things that go wrong that don't always get fixed or get put back together the way they were before. I've learned that some broken things stay broken, and I've learned that you can get through bad times and keep looking for better ones, as long as you have people who love you. From *Good in Bed*

Oprah Winfrey

If you want your life to be more rewarding, you have to change the way you think.

LISTENING

Karl A. Menninger

Listening is a magnetic and strange thing, a creative force. The friends who listen to us are the ones we move toward. When we are listened to, it creates us, makes us unfold and expand.

LISTENING TO YOURSELF

Marian Wright Edelman

Learn to be quiet enough to hear the sound of the genuine within yourself so that you can hear it in others.

LITTLE VERSUS BIG

August Strindberg

Life is not so idiotically mathematical that only the big eat the small; it is just as common for a bee to kill a lion or at least to drive it mad.

William Wordsworth

That best portion of a good man's life, his little, nameless, unremembered acts of kindness and love.

LONDON

Groucho Marx

I'm leaving because the weather is too good. I hate London when it's not raining.

LOSS

Author Unknown

He who loses money, loses much; he who loses a friend, loses much more; he who loses faith, loses all.

Dean Koontz

Because God is never cruel, there is a reason for all things. We must know the pain of loss; because if we never knew it, we would have no compassion for others, and we would become monsters of self-regard, creatures of unalloyed self-interest. The terrible pain of loss teaches humility to our prideful kind, has the power to soften uncaring hearts, to make a better person of a good one. From *The Darkest Evening of the Year*

Edna St. Vincent Millay

I only know that summer sang in me A little while, that in me sings no more.

LOVE

Jane Austen

In vain have I struggled. It will not do. My feelings will not be repressed. You must allow me to tell you how ardently I admire and love you. From *Pride and Prejudice*

Jane Austen

You have bewitched me in body and soul, and I love, I love, I love you. I never wish to be parted with you from this day on. Spoken by Mr. Darcy in *Pride and Prejudice*

Louis de Bernières

Love is a temporary madness, it erupts like volcanoes and then subsides. And when it subsides, you have to make a decision. You have to work out whether your roots have so entwined together that it is inconceivable that you should ever part. Because that is what love is. Love is not breathlessness, it is not excitement, it is not promulgation of promises of eternal passion, it is not desire to mate every second minute of the day, it is not lying awake at night imagining that he is kissing every cranny of your body. No, don't blush, I am telling you some truths. That is just being "in love," which any fool can do. Love itself is what is left over when being in love has burned away, and this is both an art and a fortunate accident. From *Captain Corelli's Mandolin*

John Dryden

Love reckons hours for months, and days for years; And every little absence is an age.

Alan Jay Lerner

I've grown accustomed ... to her face. From *My Fair Lady*

Rick Riordan

And," Annabeth continued, "it reminds me how long we've known each other. We were twelve, Percy. Can you believe that?" "No, he admitted. "So ... you knew you liked me from that moment?" She smirked. "I hated you at first. You annoyed me. Then I tolerated you for a few years. Then —" "Okay, fine." She leaned in and kissed him a good, proper kiss without anyone watching — no Romans anywhere, no screaming satyr chaperones. She pulled away. "I missed you, Percy." Percy wanted to tell her the same thing, but it seemed too small a comment. While he had been on the Roman side, he'd kept himself alive almost solely by thinking of Annabeth. I missed you didn't really cover that. From *The Mark of Athena*

Marjory Heath Wentworth

The weight of love is the heaviest burden.

MARRIAGE

Madeleine L'Engle

If we commit ourselves to one person for life, this is not, as many people think, a rejection of freedom; rather, it demands the courage to move into all the risks of freedom, and the risk of love which is permanent; into that love which is not possession but participation.

Madeleine L'Engle

No long-term marriage is made easily, and there have been times when I've been so angry or so hurt that I thought my love would never recover. And then, in the midst of near despair, something has happened beneath the surface. A bright little flashing fish of hope has flicked silver fins and the water is bright and suddenly I am returned to a state of love again — till next time. I've learned that there will always be a next time, and that I will submerge in darkness and misery, but that I won't stay submerged. And each time something has been learned under the waters; something has been gained; and a new kind of love has grown. The best I can ask for is that this love, which has been built on countless failures, will continue to grow. I can say no more than that this is mystery, and gift, and that somehow or other, through grace, our failures can be redeemed and blessed.

William Shakespeare

God, the best maker of all marriages, combine your hearts in one.

THE MEASURE OF A PERSON

Martin Luther King, Jr.

The ultimate measure of a man is not where he stands in moments of comfort and convenience, but where he stands at times of challenge and controversy.

MEEK

Max Lucado

"Blessed are the meek," Jesus said. The word meek does not mean weak. It means focused. It is a word used to describe a domesticated stallion. Power under control. Strength with direction. From *In the Eye of the Storm*

MEMORY

George Cooper

Sweet Genevieve, The days may come, the days may go, But will the hands of memory weave, The blissful dreams of long ago. From *Sweet Genevieve*

William Shakespeare

The windows of mine eyes. From *King Richard III, Act V, sciii*

MEN AND WOMEN

John Gray

When a man can listen to a woman's feelings without getting angry and frustrated, he gives her a wonderful gift. He makes it safe for her to express herself. The more she is able to express herself, the more she feels heard and understood, and the more she is able to give a man the loving trust, acceptance, appreciation, admiration, approval, and encouragement that he needs. From *Men Are from Mars, Women Are from Venus*

Goldie Hawn

There are only three ages for women in Hollywood — Babe, District Attorney, and Driving Miss Daisy.

Jean Kerr

Women speak because they wish to speak, whereas a man speaks only when driven to speech by something outside himself — like, for instance, he can't find any clean socks.

Richard Brinsley Sheridan

Through all the drama — whether damned or not — Love gilds the scene, and women guide the plot. From *The Rivals*

Frederick Salomon Perls

I do my thing, and you do your thing ... You are you and I am I, And if by chance we find each other, it's beautiful; If not, it can't be helped. From *Gestalt Therapy Verbatim*

MIND

Leonardo da Vinci

Iron rusts from disuse; stagnant water loses its purity and in cold weather becomes frozen; even so does inaction sap the vigor of the mind.

Nancy Nordenson

The mind one uses and adds to all the days of one's life is not unlike a building ... but to build it functional and fine and soaring, one must first put in place a supporting framework ... the mind's scaffold needs a spiritual construction. Beams of truth to hold the weight of everything else. From *Just Think: Nourish Your Mind to Feed Your Soul*

MOMENTS

Gwendolyn Brooks

Exhaust the little moment. Soon it dies. And be it gash or gold it will not come again in this identical disguise. From *Exhaust the Little Moment*

Sonia Cafe

Each moment is an opportunity to reveal a miracle. Grace is a wonderful quality of the Spirit. When it is manifested in our lives, it brings the energy that uplifts our vibrations and clears the inner barriers. To be in a state of gratefulness is to put into practice the certainty that if we knock the door will be opened, and if we ask it will be given unto us.

MONEY

Thomas Fuller

It is better to have a hen tomorrow than an egg today.

MOON

Doc Jonathan

To make such an attempt as to hold the rays of the sun in one's palm, such would be the pair to wisps of moon beams caught on the rising tide of starlight.

Edward Lear

They dined on mince, and slices of quince, Which they ate with a runcible spoon; And hand in hand, on the edge of the sand, They danced by the light of the moon. From *The Owl and the Pussycat*

MORNING

Jean Kerr

The average, healthy, well-adjusted adult gets up at seven-thirty in the morning feeling just plain terrible.

MOTHERING

Barbara Kingsolver

There were two things about Mama. One is she always expected the best out of me. And the other is that then no matter what I did, whatever I came home with, she acted like it was the moon I had just hung up in the sky and plugged in all the stars. Like I was that good. From *The Bean Trees*

MUSIC

Yo Yo Ma

As you begin to realize that every different type of music, everybody's individual music, has its own rhythm, life, language and heritage, you realize how life changes, and you learn how to be more open and adaptive to what is around us.

John Muir

The water in music the oar forsakes. The air in music the wing forsakes. All things move in music and write it. The mouse, the lizard, and grasshopper sing together on the Turlock sands, sing with the morning stars. From *Letter to Jeanne C. Carr, Yosemite*

Adelaide Anne Procter

Seated one day at the organ, I was weary and ill at ease, And my fingers wandered idly, Over the noisy keys. But I struck one chord of music, Like the sound of a great Amen.

Hunter S. Thompson

Music has always been a matter of Energy to me, a question of Fuel. Sentimental people call it Inspiration, but what they really mean is Fuel. I have always needed Fuel. I am a serious consumer. On some nights I still believe that a car with the gas needle on empty can run about fifty more miles if you have the right music very loud on the radio.

NEW YEAR

G. K. Chesterton

The object of a new year is not that we should have a new year. It is that we should have a new soul.

Neil Gaiman

May your coming year be filled with magic and dreams and good madness. I hope you read some fine books and kiss someone who thinks you're wonderful, and don't forget to make some art — write or draw or build or sing or live as only you can. And I hope, somewhere in the next year, you surprise yourself.

NEW YEAR'S DAY

Charles Lamb

New Year 's Day is every man's birthday.

NOISE

Julian Treasure

The world is now so noisy with this cacophony going on visually and auditorily, it's just hard to listen; it's tiring to listen.

NONSENSE

Dr. Suess

I like nonsense, it wakes up the brain cells. Fantasy is a necessary ingredient in living.

OBSTACLES

Molière

The greater the obstacle the more glory in overcoming it.

OPTIMISM

Walt Disney

It's kind of fun to do the impossible.

Vince Lombardi

We didn't lose the game; we just ran out of time.

OUR IMAGE

Augustine

You made us for Yourself, and our hearts find no peace until they rest in You.

OVER IMAGINING

Kate Morton

She was curious by nature, Mother had always said so. She'd shaken her head and clicked her tongue, and told Eliza that if she didn't learn to stop her mind racing on ahead of her she'd end up running into a mountain made of her imaginings. From *The Forgotten Garden*

PAIN

Pain is a gift no one wants. — Church billboard

PARIS

Ernest Hemingway

If you are lucky enough to have lived in Paris as a young man, then wherever you go for the rest of your life, it stays with you, for Paris is a moveable feast. From *A Moveable Feast*

PARTIES

F. Scott Fitzgerald

And I like large parties. They're so intimate. At small parties there isn't any privacy. From *The Great Gatsby*

PEOPLE

Marian Anderson

As long as you keep a person down, some part of you has to be down there to hold him down, so it means you cannot soar as you otherwise might.

Elisabeth Kübler-Ross

People are like stained-glass windows. They sparkle and shine when the sun is out, but when the darkness sets in, their true beauty is revealed only if there is a light from within.

Madea Goes to Jail

If somebody wants to walk out of your life, let them go! Some people are meant to come into your life for a lifetime, some for only a season and you got to know which is which. And you're always messing up when you mix those seasonal people up with lifetime expectations.

Sir Isaac Newton

If I can see further, it's because I've stood on the shoulders of giants.

Plato

People are like dirt. They can either nourish you and help you grow as a person or they can stunt your growth and make you wilt and die.

Mister Rogers

I wonder if you don't have someone in your life that just the very thought of that person makes you feel better.

Hilary T. Smith

People are like cities: We all have alleys and gardens and secret rooftops and places where daisies sprout between the sidewalk cracks, but most of the time all we let each other see is a postcard glimpse of a skyline or a polished square. Love lets you find those hidden places in another person, even the ones they didn't know were there, even the ones they wouldn't have thought to call beautiful themselves.

PERSEVERANCE

Samuel Johnson

Great works are performed not by strength but by perseverance.

PERSISTENCE

Confucius

In the battle between the river and the rock, the river will always win. Not through strength but by persistence.

PHILOSOPHY

Norman Geisler

A student asked in Philosophy, "How do I know that I exist?" Dr. Norman replied, "and whom shall I say is asking?"

POINT OF VIEW

Winston Churchill

A pessimist sees the difficulty in every opportunity, an optimist sees the opportunity in every difficulty.

POSSIBILITARIAN

Norman Vincent Peale

Become a possibilitarian. No matter how dark things seem to be or actually are, raise your sights and see the possibilities — always see them, for they're always there.

POSSIBILITY

Jodi Hills

Realizing how much this dream could change her life, her life already started to change.

Golda Meir

Trust yourself. Create the kind of self you will be happy to live with all your life. Make the most of yourself by fanning the tiny, inner sparks of possibility into flames of achievement.

POVERTY

Jean Kerr

You don't seem to realize that a poor person who is unhappy is in a better position than a rich person who is unhappy. Because, the poor person has hope. He or she thinks money would help.

PRAYER

Reinhold Niebuhr

God, give us grace to accept with serenity the things that cannot be changed, courage to change the things which should be changed, and the wisdom to distinguish the one from the other. From *The Serenity Prayer*

Leonard Sweet

Help me, Lord, to receive what You give: give all You ask; ask what You desire; desire all You require. Amen.

PRIDE

Mary Shelley

"Man," I cried, "how ignorant art thou in thy pride of wisdom!" From *Frankenstein*

PROCRASTINATION

Julia Cameron

At root, procrastination is an investment in fantasy. We are waiting for that mysterious and elusive moment when we will work perfectly.

PURPOSE

Richard Bach

Here is a test to find out whether your mission in life is complete. If you're alive, it isn't. From *Illusions*

Rosalind Russell

Life is a banquet, and most poor suckers are starving to death.

READING

Dr. Suess

The more that you read, the more things you will know. The more that you learn, the more places you'll go.

REALITY BITES

Samson Raphaelson

Playwright Samson Raphaelson told about his hitting it rich and buying a yacht and going, in a peaked cap, to see his old Jewish mother. She asked him what the cap was for. "It's my captain's hat, Mama," he said. "I'm a captain." She nodded "By me, you're a captain," she said. "And by you, you're a captain. But by captains, you're no captain."

RELATIONSHIPS

Rick Warren

God sometimes removes a person from your life for your protection. Don't run after them.

REPUBLIC

Alexis de Tocqueville

The American Republic will endure until the day Congress discovers that it can bribe the public with the public's money.

RESENTMENT

Max Lucado

Resentment is the cocaine of the emotions. From *The Applause of Heaven*

REVENGE

Max Lucado

Revenge is the raging fire that consumes the arsonist.

RISK TAKING

William Shedd

A ship in the harbor is safe, but that is not what ships are built for.

RUNNING AWAY

Dawn Clifton Tripp

. . .she could sense his flight – how he tried to dart and dodge his grief – she could sense his albatross wings. From *Moontide*

SAFENESS

Clyde Cook

Clyde Cook, former president of Biola University grew up in a missionary family in China at a time of the Japanese occupation. He told of the great fear he had during nighttime travels. His mother said, "Clyde, safety is not the absence of danger; It is the presence of God."

SAINT PATRICK'S DAY

Adrienne Cook

St. Patrick's Day is an enchanted time — a day to begin transforming winter's dreams into summer's magic.

SALVATION

Longfellow could take a worthless sheet of paper, write a poem on it, and make it worth $6,000 — that's genius. Rockefeller could sign his name to a piece of paper and make it worth a million dollars — that's capital. Uncle Sam can take gold, stamp an eagle on it, and make it worth $50 — that's money. A mechanic can take material that is worth only $5 and make it worth $50 — that's skill. An artist can take a piece of canvas, paint a picture on it, and make it worth $1,000 — that's art. God can take a worthless, sinful life, wash it in the blood of Christ, put His Spirit in it, and make it a blessing to humanity — that's salvation. — From *Christian Digest*

SAND

Author Unknown

Write your hurts in the sand and etch your blessings on stone.

Max Lucado

There is only so much sand in the hourglass.

SATISFACTION

Epicurus

He who is not satisfied with a little, is satisfied with nothing.

William Shakespeare

He is well paid that is well satisfied.

SEA

I'm going to the beach and I'm going to stay forever ... I'll wear flip flops and a bathing suit and that's all! I'll smile all the time and dance in the sun. "Don't bother me, I'm relaxing," I'll say. I'll nap and read all the books I never have time to read. I'll walk on the sand and get really smooth feet, then I'll paint my toenails a color called "Endless summer pink." I'll get beautiful tan lines and I'll be so thankful!" — Written on a pillow at a vacation home in Poipu Sands, Kauai, Hawaii

Louisa May Alcott

I am not afraid of storms, for I am learning how to sail my ship.

Dave Barry

There's nothing wrong with enjoying looking at the surface of the ocean itself, except that when you finally see what goes on underwater, you realize that you've been missing the whole point of the ocean. Staying on the surface all the time is like going to the circus and staring at the tent.

Oswald Chambers

The call of God is like the call of the sea, no one hears it but the one who has the nature of the sea in him. From *The Baffling Call of God*

Isak Dinesen

The cure for anything is salt water – sweat, tears or the sea.

Sarah Kay

Because there's nothing more beautiful than the way the ocean refuses to stop kissing the shoreline, no matter how many times it's sent away.

Herman Melville

You must have plenty of sea-room to tell the truth in.

Julian Treasure

[Ocean surf] has the frequency of roughly 12 cycles per minute. And ... 12 cycles per minute is [also] roughly the frequency of the breathing of a sleeping human. There is a deep resonance with being at rest.

SELF-ESTEEM

ChocoWit saying

Fishing for compliments keeps the real ones at bay.

Henri J.M. Nouwen

Over the years, I have come to realize that the greatest trap in our life is not success, popularity, or power, but self-rejection. Success, popularity, and power can indeed present a great temptation, but their seductive quality often comes from the way they are part of the much larger temptation to self-rejection. When we have come to believe in the voices that call us worthless and unlovable, then success, popularity, and power are easily perceived as attractive solutions. The real trap, however, is self-rejection. As soon as someone accuses me or criticizes me, as soon as I am rejected, left alone, or abandoned, I find myself thinking, "Well, that proves once again that I am a nobody." ... [My dark side says,] I am no good ... I deserve to be pushed aside, forgotten, rejected, and abandoned. Self-rejection is the greatest enemy of the spiritual life because it contradicts the sacred voice that calls us the "Beloved." Being the Beloved constitutes the core truth of our existence.

SELF-PITY

Maya Angelou

Self-pity in its early stage is as snug as a feather mattress; only when it hardens does it become uncomfortable.

SELF-SUFFICIENCY

Louis Brandeis

No one can really pull you up very high — you lose your grip on the rope. But on your own two feet you can climb mountains.

SHAME

Brené Brown

Shame corrodes the very part of us that believes we are capable of change. From *I Thought It Was Just Me: Women Reclaiming Power and Courage in a Culture of Shame*

Charles Dickens

Heaven knows we need never be ashamed of our tears, for they are rain upon the blinding dust of earth, overlying our hard hearts. I was better after I had cried, than before — more sorry, more aware of my own ingratitude, more gentle. From *Great Expectations*

Kimberly Giles

The world needs you to let go of self-pity and shame regarding your life experiences, too. The world needs you to use the things you have learned for good. Stop letting your past mistakes define you and affect your value. Let go of separation and victimhood and find meaning in what you have been through. From *Choosing Clarity: The Path to Fearlessness*

Jonathan Swift

I never wonder to see men wicked, but I often wonder to see them not ashamed.

SHELLS AND SHINY OBJECTS

Anne Morrow Lindbergh

One can collect only a few [shells], and those are more beautiful if they are few.

Christy Tryhus

Stop following every bright and shiny object. Stay in your swim lane.

SITUATIONS

Helen Schucman

Every situation, properly perceived, becomes an opportunity.

SNOW

Lewis Carroll

I wonder if the snow loves the trees and fields, that it kisses them so gently? And then it covers them up snug, you know, with a white quilt; and perhaps it says "Go to sleep, darlings, till the summer comes again." From *Alice's Adventures in Wonderland and Through the Looking-Glass*

SOUL

C. S. Lewis

This signature on each soul may be a product of heredity and environment, but that only means that heredity and environment are among the instruments whereby God creates a soul. I am considering not how, but why, He makes each soul unique. If He had no use for all these differences, I do not see why He should have created more souls than one. Be sure that the ins and outs of your individuality are no mystery to Him; and one day they will no longer be a mystery to you ...

Your soul has a curious shape because it is a hollow made to fit a particular swelling in the infinite contours of the Divine substance, or a key to unlock one of the doors in the house with many mansions. For it is not humanity in the abstract that is to be saved, but you — you, the individual reader, John Stubbs or Janet Smith. Blessed and fortunate creature, your eyes shall behold Him and not another's. All that you are, sins apart, is destined, if you will let God have His good way, to utter satisfaction. The Brocken spectre "looked to every man like his first love," because she was a cheat. But God will look to every soul like its first love because He is its first love. Your place in heaven will seem to be made for you and you alone, because you were made for it — made for it stitch by stitch as a glove is made for a hand. From *The Problem of Pain*

Herbert Trench Shakespeare

A circumnavigator of the soul.

A. W. Tozer

Your poor heart, in which God put appreciation for everlastingness, will not take electronic gadgets in lieu of eternal life. Something inside of you is too big for that, too terrible, too wonderful. God has set everlastingness in your heart. All the things of this world are here for but a moment and then are gone. None can satisfy the longing for that eternal ragging in the soul of every man. From *And He Dwelt Among Us: Teachings from the Gospel of John*

SOUND

Julian Treasure

Birdsong is a sound which most people find reassuring. There is a reason for that. ... we've learned that when the birds are singing, things are safe. It's when they stop you need to be worried.

SPRING

Algernon Charles Swinburne

For winter's rains and ruins are over, And all the season of snows and sins; The days dividing lover and lover, The light that loses, the night that wins; And time remembered is grief forgotten, And frosts are slain and flowers begotten, And in green underwood and cover, Blossom by blossom the spring begins. From *Atalanta in Calydon*

Algernon Charles Swinburne

If you were April's lady, And I were lord in May. From *A Match*

STAR-DUST

Henry David Thoreau

If the day and the night are such that you greet them with joy, and life emits a fragrance like flowers and sweet-scented herbs, is more elastic, more starry, more immortal — that is your success. All nature is your congratulation, and you have cause momentarily to bless yourself. The greatest gains and values are farthest from being appreciated. We easily come to doubt if they exist. We soon forget them. They are the highest reality. Perhaps the facts most astounding and most real are never communicated by man to man. The true harvest of my daily life is somewhat as intangible and indescribable as the tints of morning or evening. It is a little star-dust caught, a segment of the rainbow which I have clutched. From *Walden*

STUMBLING

Author Unknown

Every path has its puddle.

Thomas Fuller

A stumble may prevent a fall.

SUCCESS

Alexandre Dumas

Nothing succeeds like success.

The Layman Reflections on the Revolution of France

The most opposite passions necessarily succeed.

Louis L'Amour

To be successful you need to gain a little ground, hold, gain a little ground, hold it.

SUFFERING

Joy DeKok

We give our suffering value when we write our way into healing. We pass that healing on when we share it in our legacies. From *Your Life A Legacy*

SUMMER

Albert Camus

In the depths of winter, I finally learned that within me there lay an invincible summer.

Lucy Stone

I expect some new phase of life this summer and shall try to get the honey from each moment.

William Wordsworth

. . .One of those heavenly days that cannot die.

TIMBRE

F. Scott Fitzgerald

It was the kind of voice that the ear follows up and down, as if each speech is an arrangement of notes that will never be played again. From *The Great Gatsby*

TIME

Albert Einstein

The only reason for time is so that everything doesn't happen at once.

C. S. Lewis

The Future is something which everyone reaches at the rate of sixty minutes an hour, whatever he does, whoever he is. From *The Screwtape Letters*

Earl Nightingale

Don't let the fear of the time it will take to accomplish something stand in the way of your doing it. The time will pass anyway; we might just as well put that passing time to the best possible use.

Marcel Proust

The time which we have at our disposal every day is elastic; the passions that we feel expand it, those that we inspire contract it; and habit fills up what remains From *Within a Budding Grove*

TODAY

Author Unknown

A kindness done today is the surest way to a brighter tomorrow.

Ralph Waldo Emerson

Write it on your heart that every day is the best day in the year.

Jodi Hills

It isn't that something comes along and gives you a reason to get out of bed ... you have to get out of bed and go find that reason — every day!

Steve Jobs

For the past thirty-three years, I have looked in the mirror every morning and asked myself: "If today were the last day of my life, would I want to do what I am about to do today?"' And whenever the answer has been "No" for too many days in a row, I know I need to change something.

Groucho Marx

I, not events, have the power to make me happy or unhappy today. I can choose which it shall be. Yesterday is dead, tomorrow hasn't arrived yet. I have just one day, today, and I'm going to be happy in it.

Cecil Murphey

This is the best I can do at this stage of my development.

Jim Rohn

Either you run the day or the day runs you.

Eleanor Roosevelt

With the new day comes new strength and new thoughts.

Robert Louis Stevenson

Don't judge each day by the harvest you reap but by the seeds that you plant.

E. B. White

I arise in the morning torn between a desire to improve the world and a desire to enjoy the world. This makes it hard to plan the day.

William Wordsworth

Blessed mood, In which the burthen of the mystery, In which the heavy and the weary weights of all this unintelligible word, is lightened. From *Lines Composed a Few Miles Above Tintern Abbey*

William Wordsworth

Sweet childish days, that were as long, As twenty days are now. From *To a Butterfly*

TOMORROW

Brad Paisley

Tomorrow is the first blank page of a 365-page book. Write a good one.

Lauren Oliver

Tomorrow. Maybe for you there's one thousand tomorrows, or three thousand, or ten, so much time you can bathe in it, roll around in it, let it slide like coins through your fingers. So much time you can waste it. But for some of us there's only today. And the truth is, you never really know. From *Before I Fall*

TRAVEL

Agatha Christie

Trains are wonderful ... To travel by train is to see nature and human beings, towns and churches and rivers, in fact, to see life.

Ernest Hemingway

Never go on trips with anyone you do not love. From *A Moveable Feast*

TRUST

Oswald Chambers

Trust God and take the next step.

UNCERTAINTY

An Old Cornish Hymn

I know not what the future has, of marvel or surprise, Assured alone that life and death His mercy underlies. And if my heart and faith are weak to bear an untried pain; A bruised reed He will not break, but strengthen and sustain.

UNITY

Augustine

Unity in essentials, freedom in non-essentials, love in everything.

UNIVERSE

Alfred Lord Tennyson

I am a part of all that I have met.

VEGETARIAN

Groucho Marx

I'm not a vegetarian, but I eat animals who are.

VISIONS AND DREAMS

Napoleon Hill

Cherish your visions and your dreams as they are the children of your soul; the blueprints of your ultimate achievements.

WARNING SIGNS

Christopher Morley

There was so much handwriting on the wall that even the wall fell down. From *Around the Clock*

WEALTH

Robert Collier

All riches have their origin in mind. Wealth is in ideas — not money.

WEEPING

Golda Meir

Those who don't know how to weep with their whole heart, don't know how to laugh either. — Former Prime Minister of Israel

WHO WE ARE

T. R. Kelly

We are trying to be several selves at once, without all ourselves being organized by a single, mastering life within us. Each of us tends to be, not a single self, but a whole committee of selves. There is a civic self, the parental self, the financial self, the religious self, the society self, the professional self, the literary self. And each of our selves in turn a rank individualist, not cooperative but shooting out his votes loudly for himself when the voting comes.

WHY I AM HERE

Winston Churchill

What is the use of living, if it be not to strive for noble causes and to make this muddled world a better place for those who will live after we are gone?

WINE

Galileo

Wine is sunlight in a glass.

Dom Perignon

Come quickly, I'm drinking stars.

Minnesota Wine website

Grape minds think alike.

Robert Louis Stevenson

Wine is bottled poetry.

WISDOM

Socrates

The only true wisdom is in knowing you know nothing.

WIT

Dorothy Parker

Wit has truth in it; wisecracking is simply calisthenics with words.
From *In the Paris Review*

WONDER

Eberhard Arnold

Only those who look with the eyes of children can lose themselves in the object of their wonder.

Louis Pasteur

"... to wonder and question is the first step of the mind toward discovery.

WORDS

Elie Wiesel

Words can sometimes, in moments of grace, attain the quality of deeds.

WORSHIP

Gordon Dahl

Most middle-class Americans tend to worship their work, to work at their play, and to play at their worship.

WRITING

Anton Chekhov

What is needed is constant work, day and night, constant reading, study, will ... Every hour is precious for it. You must drop your vanity. You are not a child. It is time. — To a young writer who wanted advice

Clarence Darrow

Someday I hope to write a book where the royalties will pay for the copies I give away.

Peter DeVries

I like being a writer. What I can't stand is the paperwork.

Joyce K. Ellis

Write so Heaven looks different because of what you wrote on earth. Don't listen to the critic. Write for the heart.

Ben Franklin

Either write something worth reading or do something worth writing.

Ira Glass

Nobody tells this to people who are beginners, I wish someone told me. All of us who do creative work, we get into it because we have good taste. But there is this gap. For the first couple years you make stuff, it's just not that good. It's trying to be good, it has potential, but it's not. But your taste, the thing that got you into the game, is still killer. And your taste is why your work disappoints you. A lot of people never get past this phase, they quit. Most people I know who do interesting, creative work went through years of this. We know our work doesn't have this special thing that we want it to have. We all go through this. And if you are just starting out or you are still in this phase, you gotta know it's normal and the most important thing you can do is do a lot of work. Put yourself on a deadline so that every week you will finish one story. It is only by going through a volume of work that you will close that gap, and your work will be as good as your ambitions. And I took longer to figure out how to do this than anyone I've ever met. It's gonna take awhile. It's normal to take awhile. You've just gotta fight your way through.

Nathaniel Hawthorne

Easy reading is very hard writing.

Nancy Kress

Give yourself artificial deadlines. Tell yourself, "I will mail this story by April 3 (or May 14, or August 8)." Tell everyone else, too; fellow workshop participants, your spouse, your mother, your kids. Ask them to ask you whether the story's gone out. Make it such a big deal that you must finish polishing or you'll feel like the biggest fool in the world.

Madeleine L'Engle

Our truest response to the irrationality of the world is to paint or sing or write, for only in such response do we find truth.

Henry Miller

You have to write a million words before you find your voice as a writer.

Grace Paley

Write what will stop your breath if you don't write.

Blaise Pascal

I would have written a shorter letter, but I did not have the time.

Joseph Pulitzer

Put it before them briefly so they will read it, clearly so they will appreciate it, picturesquely so they will remember it, and above all, accurately so they will be guided by its light.

Rainer Maria Rilke

Everything is gestation and then bringing forth. To let each impression and each germ of a feeling come to completion wholly in itself, in the dark, in the inexpressible, the unconscious, beyond the reach of one's own intelligence, and await with deep humility and patience the birth-hour of a new clarity: that alone is living the artist's life: in understanding as in creating.

William Shakespeare

An honest tale speeds best being plainly told.

John Steinbeck

And now that you don't have to be perfect, you can be good.

John Millington Synge

When I was writing *The Shadow of the Glen* I got more aid than any learning could have given me from a chink in the floor of the old Wicklow house where I was staying, that let me hear what was being said by the servant girls in the kitchen.

YOU

Maya Angelou

You alone, are enough.

Augustine

Seek not to understand that you may believe, but believe that you may understand.

Oswald Chambers

Be absolutely His.

E. E. Cummings

To be nobody but myself in a world that is doing its best, night and day, to make you everybody else, means to fight the hardest battle which any human being can fight, and never stop fighting.

T. S. Eliot

Do I dare disturb the universe?

Leighton Ford

God loves us the way we are, but He loves us too much to leave us that way.

Viktor Frankl

Not only our experiences, but all we have done, whatever great thoughts we may have had, and all we have suffered, all this is not lost, though it is past; we brought it into being. Having been is also a kind of being, and perhaps the surest kind. From *Man's Search for Meaning*

Rev. Richard C. Halverson

You go nowhere by accident. Wherever you go, God is sending you. Wherever you are, God has put you there. He has a purpose in your being there. Christ who dwells within you has something He wants to do through you where you are. Believe this and go in His grace and love and power. — Former Chaplain of the U. S. Senate

Sophia Loren

Getting ahead in a difficult profession — singing, acting, writing, whatever — requires avid faith in yourself. You must be able to sustain yourself against staggering blows and unfair reversals. When I think back to those first couple of years in Rome, those endless rejections, without a glimmer of encouragement from anyone, all those failed screen tests, and yet I never let my desire slide away from me, my belief in myself, and what I felt I could achieve.

Friedrich Nietzsche

That which does not kill me, makes me stronger.

John Piper

Lord, let me make a difference for You that is utterly disproportionate to who I am.

Anne Wilson Shaef

The unfolding of my life is not an issue of competence or control. It is an issue of faith.

Marjory Heath Wentworth

You have learned to carry. In the silence of the heavens, it's a dream that wakes you with the sound of your own voice singing. From *The Sound of Your Own Voice Singing*

When the Saints Go Marching In

O Lord, I want to be in that number, when the saints go marching in.
Anonymous Spiritual

Macrina Wiederkehr

O God, help me believe the truth about myself, no matter how beautiful it is.

Marianne Williamson

Our deepest fear is not that we are inadequate. Our deepest fear is that we are powerful beyond measure. It is our light, not our darkness, that most frightens us. We ask ourselves, who am I to be brilliant, gorgeous, talented, and fabulous? Actually, who are you not to be? You are a child of God. Your playing small doesn't serve the world. There's nothing enlightening about shrinking so that other people won't feel insecure around you. We are born to manifest the glory of God that is within us. It's in everyone. And as we let our own light shine, we unconsciously give other people permission to do the same. As we are liberated from our own fear, our presence automatically liberates others.

SCRIPTURE REFERENCES AS IT RELATES TO:

DARKNESS

Genesis 1:2 ESV

The earth was formless and empty, and darkness covered the deep waters. And the Spirit of God was hovering over the surface of the waters.

Psalm 139:11-12 NIV

If I say, "Surely the darkness will hide me" and the light become night around me, even the darkness will not be dark to You; the night will shine like the day for darkness is as light to You.

Isaiah 45:3 NLT

And I will give you treasures hidden in the darkness — secret riches. I will do this so that you may know that I am the Lord the God of Israel, the One who calls you by name.

FEAR

2 Chronicles 20:9 NLT

We can cry out to You to save us, and You will hear us and rescue us.

2 Timothy 1:7 NKJV

For God has not given us a spirit of fear but of power, of love, and of a sound mind.

Hebrews 6:18-19 NLT

We who have fled to Him for refuge can take new courage, for we can hold on to His promise with confidence.

FIRE STARTERS

Isaiah 50:11 NIV

But now, all you who light fires and provide yourselves with flaming torches, go, walk in the light of your fires and of the torches you have set ablaze.

GENEROSITY

2 Corinthians 9:6 NIV

Remember this: Whoever sows sparingly, will reap sparingly. And whoever sows generously will also reap generously.

GOD'S AUTHORITY OVER NATURE

Hebrews 1:7 NLT

He makes his angels wind, his servants flames of fire.

GOD'S ONLY SON

Malachi 4:2 NLT

... You who revere My name, the Sun of Righteousness will rise with healing in its wings.

GOD'S SENSE OF FAIRNESS

Hebrews 6:10 NLT

For God is not unfair. He will not forget how hard you have worked for Him and how you have shown your love to Him by caring for other Christians, as you still do.

GOD'S VIEW OF ME

Psalm 73:24 NLT

You will keep on guiding me with Your counsel, leading me to a glorious destiny.

GOD WORKING IN YOU AND ME

Philippians 2:13 NLT

For God is working in you, giving you the desire to obey Him and the power to do what pleases Him.

HOLY SPIRIT

2 Corinthians 4:7 NLT

This precious treasure — this light and power that now shine within us — is held in perishable containers, that is, in our weak bodies.

HOW GOD USES US

2 Corinthians 2:14 NLT

Wherever we go He uses us to tell others about the Lord and to spread the Good News like a sweet perfume.

Acts 20:24 NLT

But my life is worth nothing unless I use it for doing the work assigned me by the Lord Jesus — the work of telling others the Good News about God's wonderful kindness and love.

HOW TO LIVE

Romans 14:13 NLT

So let's stop condemning each other. Decide instead to live in such a way that you will not cause another believer to stumble and fall.

HUMILITY

1 Peter 5:6-7 MSG

So be content with who you are, and don't put on airs. God's strong hand is on you; He'll promote you at the right time. Live carefree before God; He is most careful with you.

LIFE

John 10:10 NLT

The thief's purpose is to steal and kill and destroy. My purpose is to give life in all its fullness.

PATIENCE

Ecclesiastes 7:8 NLT

Patience is better than pride.

PERSEVERANCE

1 Corinthians 15:58 NLT

Be strong and immovable ... for you know that nothing you do for the Lord is ever useless.

PLUMB LINE

Psalm 33:4 MSG

For God's Word is solid to the core; everything He makes is sound inside and out. He loves it when everything fits, when His world is in plumb-line true. Earth is drenched in God's affectionate satisfaction.

PRIDE VERSUS HUMILITY

Proverbs 29:23 NLT

Pride ends in humiliation, while humility brings honor.

PROVISION

Matthew 6:33 NLT

He will give you all you need from day to day if you live for Him and make the Kingdom of God your primary concern.

ROCK THEMES

1 Peter 2:5 NLT

And you are living stones that God is building into His spiritual temple.

Revelation 2:17 NLT

I will give to each one a white stone, and on the stone will be engraved a new name that no one will know except the one who receives it.

SEA OR WATER

Isaiah 51:10 NIV

... Who made a road in the depths of the sea.

Ecclesiastes 1:7 NIV

All the streams flow into the sea yet the sea is never full.

SEASONS

Song of Songs 2:11-12 NIV

See! The winter is past; the rains are over and gone. Flowers appear on the earth; the season of singing has come, the cooing of doves is heard in our land.

STATION IN LIFE

Psalm 40:2 NLT

He set my feet on solid ground and steadied me as I walked along.

2 Corinthians 12:10 NLT

Since I know it is all for Christ's good, I am quite content with my weaknesses and with insults, hardships, persecutions, and calamities. For when I am weak, then I am strong.

TIME

Ephesians 5:16-17 NASB

Mak[e] the most of your time, because the days are evil. So then do not be foolish, but understand what the will of the Lord is.

WHAT GOD SAYS ABOUT ME

Psalm 139:16 NIV

All the days ordained for me were written in Your book before one of them came to be.

WHEN WE SEEK HIM

Malachi 3:6-7 NIV

I the Lord do not change ... Return to Me, and I will return to you, says the Lord Almighty.

WHICH PATH TO TAKE

Jeremiah 6:16 NIV

Stand at the crossroads and look; ask for the ancient paths, ask where the good way is, and walk in it, and you will find rest for your souls.

WIND

Song of Songs 4:16 RSV

Awake, north wind, and come, south wind! Blow on my garden, that its fragrance may spread abroad.

WRITING

Revelations 1:19 NLT

Write down what you have seen, both the things that are happening now and the things that will happen later.

KISSING THE SHORELINE

JULIE SAFFRIN

Index of Quotes by Subject

JULIE SAFFRIN

JULIE SAFFRIN

Index of Quotes By Author and Scripture Reference

JULIE SAFFRIN

ABOUT THE AUTHOR

JULIE SAFFRIN is the author of *Kissing the Shoreline: Quotes and Reflections to Live By* and *BlessBack®: Thank Those Who Shaped Your Life*. She received her bachelor's degree in Print Journalism and English from the University of St. Thomas. She divides her time between her home in Minneapolis, Minnesota, and her Adirondack chair at the lake in Ottertail County. Visit her at http://juliesaffrin.com.

A WORD FROM JULIE

I hope you enjoyed *Kissing the Shoreline: Quotes and Reflections to Live By*. I would love to hear from you on the contact form at http://juliesafrin.com about the quotes that inspire you.

If you enjoyed *Kissing the Shoreline: Quotes and Reflections to Live By*, you will enjoy *BlessBack®: Thank Those Who Shaped Your Life*, my book on gratitude, available at Amazon.com or by order from your favorite book retailer.